D0529385

African-American Heroes

Oprah Winfrey

Stephen Feinstein

Enslow Elementary
an imprint of

Enslow Publishers, Inc.
40 Industrial Road
Box 398
Berkeley Heights, NJ 07922
USA
http://www.enslow.com

Words to Know

anchorwoman—A woman who reads the news on TV.

interview—To question someone.

nominate—To recommend someone for an honor or office.

strict—Having strong rules that must be followed carefully.

Enslow Elementary, an imprint of Enslow Publishers, Inc.

Enslow Elementary® is a registered trademark of Enslow Publishers, Inc.

Library of Congress Cataloging-in-Publication Data

Feinstein, Stephen.
    Oprah Winfrey / Stephen Feinstein.
        p. cm. — (African-American heroes)
    Includes index.
    ISBN-13: 978-0-7660-2764-0
    ISBN-10: 0-7660-2764-3   3743 2696 4/08
    1. Winfrey, Oprah—Juvenile literature. 2. Television personalities—Biography—Juvenile literature. 3. African American television personalities—Biography—Juvenile literature. 4. Actors—United States—Biography—Juvenile literature. 5. African American actors—Biography—Juvenile literature. I. Title.
    PN1992.4.W56F45   2008
    791.4502'8092—dc22
    [B]   2006026902

Printed in the United States of America

10 9 8 7 6 5 4 3 2 1

To Our Readers: We have done our best to make sure all Internet Addresses in this book were active and appropriate when we went to press. However, the author and the publisher have no control over and assume no liability for the material available on those Internet sites or on links to other Web sites. Any comments or suggestions can be sent by e-mail to comments@enslow.com or to the address on the back cover.

Every effort has been made to locate all copyright holders of material used in this book. If any errors or omissions have occurred, corrections will be made in future editions.

Illustration Credits: AP/Wide World, pp. 1, 2, 3, 5, 17 (top), 20, 21, back cover; Everett Collection, p. 18; Getty Images, pp. 17 (bottom), 19; Kosciusko Tourist Promotion Council, p. 7; Metropolitan Government Archives of Nashville and Davidson County, pp. 3, 8, 11, 12, 13, 14; Newschannel 5 Network/Nashville, TN, pp. 3, 15; personal collection of Oprah Winfrey, pp. 3, 6; Sara McIntosh Wooten, p. 9.

Cover Illustration: Everett Collection.

Contents

Chapter 1

The Girl Who Loved to Read Books

Oprah Winfrey was born on January 29, 1954, in Mississippi. Oprah's parents were very young and were not married. Her father, Vernon, was away in the army. Her mother, Vernita Lee, had trouble earning enough money.

When Oprah was four, Vernita moved up north to Milwaukee, Wisconsin, to find work. Oprah stayed behind on her grandparents' farm in Mississippi.

Oprah Winfrey was born into a poor family. She became one of the most successful American women ever.

Oprah's grandparents were very **strict**. Oprah had to do as she was told. She helped take care of the farm animals. She helped take care of the vegetable garden.

Oprah's grandmother, Hattie Mae Lee, taught her how to read and write. Hattie Mae took Oprah to church. At church, Oprah liked to read aloud. The people there loved to listen to Oprah. Hattie Mae was very proud of her.

Oprah worked hard on her grandparents' farm even when she was very little.

This is the church that Oprah went to with her grandmother.

In 1960, Hattie Mae became sick. Oprah was sent to live with her mother in Milwaukee.

When Vernita saw Oprah reading a book, she would tell her to stop wasting her time. "Go outside and play with the other children," she would say.

Vernon Winfrey, Oprah's father.

At school Oprah was always reading books. Her teachers encouraged her. But the other kids made fun of her because she was so smart.

Vernita often had friends staying at the house. Some of them were very mean to Oprah. She ran away from home more than once. She did not feel safe there.

Oprah was unhappy at home. She often stayed out late at night and got into trouble.

In 1968, when Oprah was fourteen, Vernita sent her to live with her father. Vernon Winfrey and his wife, Zelma, lived in Nashville, Tennessee.

This is Vernon Winfrey's barbershop in Nashville.

Chapter 2 Oprah's New Home

Vernon Winfrey loved his daughter. He and his new wife, Zelma, took good care of Oprah. They were strict. Oprah knew she had to obey the rules.

Zelma made sure that Oprah read a lot of books. She made sure that Oprah always did her homework.

Oprah was happy to be living with her father and stepmother. She did well in high school. She joined the public speaking club. She gave speeches in school. She gave speeches to church groups. And she took part in speaking contests. She liked to speak about equal rights for women and African Americans.

After she moved in with her father, Oprah did well in school. In this picture, she is in the middle of the front row.

Oprah and her boyfriend, Anthony Otey.

In her senior year, Oprah won a few beauty contests and got money for college. She got a job on the weekends reading the news at a radio station in Nashville. People liked listening to Oprah's voice on the radio. Oprah was voted "Most Popular Girl" when she graduated from high school.

Oprah won a contest to be Miss Fire Prevention in Nashville.

Chapter 3

Oprah Becomes a TV News Anchorwoman

Oprah started college at Tennessee State University in 1971. Her favorite classes were drama and speech. In 1973, Oprah was hired to work as a TV news anchorwoman. She became the first African-American anchorwoman and the youngest reporter on a Nashville TV station.

This picture was taken when Oprah was a high school senior.

At nineteen, Oprah was the youngest person to read the news on Nashville television.

In 1976, Oprah moved to Baltimore, Maryland. She worked as a news anchorwoman on television. Two years later, she began working on a morning TV show called *People Are Talking*. People loved the way Oprah interviewed the guests. The show was a hit.

In 1984, Oprah went to Chicago to host a TV talk show called *A.M. Chicago*. The show was very popular. Oprah was becoming famous.

Chapter 4

Oprah's Dreams Come True

Oprah had long dreamed of being a movie star. In 1984, Quincy Jones saw Oprah on her TV show. He liked her so much that he asked her to come to Hollywood to try out for a movie.

The movie was called *The Color Purple*. It was made from a book by Alice Walker. *The Color Purple* was one of Oprah's favorite books.

Oprah was chosen to play the part of Sofia. She was so good that she was nominated for an Academy Award for Best Supporting Actress. Oprah would go on to star in many more movies and TV shows.

Oprah played Sofia in the movie *The Color Purple*. She was nominated for an Academy Award.

Oprah also starred in the movie *Beloved*, with Danny Glover.

Oprah's talk show became popular with millions of people.

In 1985, Oprah's TV show was named *The Oprah Winfrey Show*. By the next year, it was shown on TV stations all over America. Soon millions of people were watching Oprah's show. Oprah won many awards for her work on TV.

Oprah's success had made her very wealthy. She wanted to do something to help others. She talked to people in the government about writing a law to protect children. In 1993, Oprah went to the White House. She saw President Bill Clinton sign the National Child Protection Act into law.

Oprah watches as President Clinton signs the National Child Protection Act.

Oprah has won many prizes and awards.

Oprah never forgot her love of books. In 1996 she started Oprah's Book Club. She talked about books on her TV show. Many Americans read the books.

In 2000, Oprah started her own magazine called O, *The Oprah Magazine.*

Now she is known to millions as simply "Oprah." Oprah Winfrey keeps trying to help people. She wants everyone to be able to reach their dreams.

Oprah Believes

The biggest adventure you can ever take is to live the life of your dreams.

Timeline

1954—Oprah is born in Mississippi on January 29.

1960—Oprah is sent to live with her mother, Vernita, in Milwaukee.

1968—Oprah is sent to live with her father, Vernon, in Nashville.

1971—Oprah reads the news at radio station WVOL in Nashville.

1973—Oprah starts working as a TV news anchorwoman at WTVF in Nashville.

1976—Oprah gets a job at WJZ-TV.

1978—Oprah begins co-hosting *People Are Talking* on WJZ.

1984—Oprah hosts the TV show *A.M. Chicago*.

1985—Oprah plays Sofia in *The Color Purple*.

1986—*The Oprah Winfrey Show* is shown all over the country.

1996—Oprah starts Oprah's Book Club.

2000—Oprah starts *O, The Oprah Magazine*.

Learn More

Books

Brown, Jonatha A. *Oprah Winfrey*. Milwaukee, Wisc.: Weekly Reader Early Learning Library, 2005.

McLeese, Don. *Oprah Winfrey*. Vero Beach, Fla.: Rourke, 2003.

Stone, Tanya Lee. *Oprah Winfrey: Success With an Open Heart*. Brookfield, Conn.: The Millbrook Press, 2001.

Web Sites

Oprah's Official Web Site

<http://www.oprah.com>

Girl Power! Guests: Academy of Achievement: Oprah Winfrey

<http://www.achievement.org>

Click on "Select Achiever," then go to "Winfrey, Oprah."

*I*ndex